Palma Travel Guide 2023

A Complete Guide on When to Go, Where to Go and What to Do in The City Of Palma

By

Randy Benjamin Webber

Copyright

Disclaimer

The author and publisher have made every effort to ensure the accuracy of the information in this publication, but they are not responsible for any errors, omissions, or different interpretations of the material.

This book is intended to educate, inform and increase awareness and understanding. The opinions and ideas expressed are solely those of the author and should not be considered expert advice or instructions. The reader is responsible for their own actions and decisions.

Table Of Contents

CHAPTER 1

INTRODUCTION

Welcome to the captivating city of Palma! This comprehensive guidebook invites you to immerse yourself in the enchanting history, breathtaking architecture, and vibrant culture of Palma, the splendid capital of the Balearic Islands in Spain. Prepare to embark on a remarkable journey through time as you explore the rich tapestry of this Mediterranean gem.

"The Palma Travel Guide" is your ultimate companion, providing a wealth of information and insider tips to help you uncover the hidden gems and iconic landmarks of this remarkable destination. From the majestic Gothic cathedral to the winding streets of the historic old town, every corner of Palma is infused with a sense of wonder and charm.

This guidebook takes you on a captivating exploration of Palma's fascinating history, from its Phoenician and Roman roots to its Moorish influences and medieval legacy. Discover the architectural wonders that grace the cityscape, such as the imposing Bellver Castle, a unique circular fortress offering panoramic views of the city, and the breathtaking Almudaina Palace, a stunning example of Moorish architecture.

Venture beyond the historical sites, and you'll find yourself immersed in the vibrant local culture of Palma. Explore the bustling markets, where the aromas of freshly baked pastries and the vibrant colors of local produce tantalize your senses. Indulge in the culinary delights of the city, from traditional tapas to innovative gastronomic creations, and savor the unique blend of Mediterranean flavors that define the local cuisine.

"Palma Travel Guide" goes beyond the city limits, inviting you to discover the natural beauty that surrounds Palma. From the crystal-clear waters of the Mediterranean Sea to the rugged mountain landscapes, there are countless opportunities for outdoor adventures. Explore the pristine beaches, hike through scenic trails, or embark on a sailing excursion to the nearby islands, and let the beauty of the Mediterranean embrace you.

Practical information is also at your fingertips, with transportation options, accommodation recommendations, and useful Spanish phrases to enhance your travel experience. Whether you're a first-time visitor to Palma or a seasoned explorer returning to uncover new treasures, "The Palma Travel Guide" is your indispensable companion, ensuring you make the most of your time in this captivating city of timeless allure. Get ready to be enchanted by the splendors of Palma!

About Palma

In this section about Palma, we will delve into revealing facts and important things to know about the place. Let's explore some interesting details:

Geography

Palma, the capital city of the Balearic Islands in Spain, is a vibrant and enchanting destination known for its stunning beaches, historic architecture, and rich cultural heritage. Located on the southern coast of the island of Mallorca, Palma boasts a fascinating geography that combines natural beauty with urban charm. Let's delve into the geography of Palma and discover what makes this Mediterranean city so special.

Geographical Location
Palma is situated on the southwestern coast of Mallorca, the largest island in the Balearic archipelago. It occupies a prime position overlooking the sparkling Mediterranean Sea. The city lies approximately 210 kilometers east of the Spanish mainland, making it easily accessible by air and sea. Its strategic location has contributed to Palma's development as a major hub for tourism and commerce in the region.

Physical Features
The landscape surrounding Palma is diverse and picturesque, characterized by a combination of coastal areas, rolling hills, and the imposing Serra de

Tramuntana mountain range. The city is nestled in a wide bay, providing a natural harbor that has played a significant role in its history.

The Coastline
Palma boasts an extensive coastline, stretching approximately 30 kilometers. The sandy beaches that fringe the city are renowned for their crystal-clear waters and golden sands. Some of the most popular beaches include Playa de Palma, Cala Major, and Illetes. These beaches offer a variety of recreational activities, such as swimming, sunbathing, and water sports.

Serra de Tramuntana
To the north of Palma lies the Serra de Tramuntana, a UNESCO World Heritage site and a prominent feature of the city's geography. This mountain range stretches along the island's northwest coast, offering breathtaking panoramic views and an abundance of outdoor activities. The highest peak in Mallorca, Puig Major, stands at 1,445 meters and is a popular destination for hikers and nature enthusiasts.

Plains And Valleys
Palma is surrounded by fertile plains and valleys that contribute to the island's agricultural productivity. The plains of Es Pla and Campos, located to the east and south of the city, are known for their fertile soils, which support the cultivation of crops such as almonds, olives, and citrus fruits. These agricultural areas also provide

picturesque landscapes of fields and orchards, adding to the charm of the region.

Urban Landscape

Within Palma itself, the geography is defined by a mix of historical and modern urban developments. The city's historic center, known as Palma Old Town, is a maze of narrow streets and ancient buildings, including the iconic La Seu Cathedral and the Almudaina Royal Palace. The waterfront promenade, Paseo Marítimo, showcases modern architecture, luxury yachts, and a vibrant nightlife scene. Palma's urban landscape seamlessly blends with its natural surroundings, creating a unique atmosphere that captivates visitors.

Climate

Since Palma is situated on the southern coast of the island of Mallorca in the western Mediterranean Sea, Its strategic location influences the climate, as it benefits from the Mediterranean Basin's mild and temperate weather. The city is shielded from extreme weather conditions by the Tramuntana Mountains to the northwest, which act as a barrier against cold winds.

Seasonal Overview

Palma experiences four distinct seasons: spring, summer, autumn, and winter. Each season brings its own unique characteristics and contributes to the overall pleasant climate of the region.

Spring (March To May)

Spring in Palma is a delightful time when the city comes to life with blossoming flowers and lush greenery. Average temperatures gradually rise during this period, ranging from 14°C (57°F) in March to 20°C (68°F) in May. Spring also sees moderate rainfall, refreshing the landscapes and providing ideal conditions for nature enthusiasts.

Summer (June To August)

Summer is the peak tourist season in Palma, thanks to its warm and sunny weather. The average temperatures during this time range between 24°C (75°F) and 30°C (86°F). The sea temperature becomes comfortably warm, making it perfect for beach activities and water sports. Rainfall is minimal during summer, with clear skies dominating the days.

Autumn (September To November)

Autumn in Palma is characterized by warm temperatures that gradually decrease as the season progresses. September still maintains summer-like weather, with temperatures averaging around 25°C (77°F). However, by November, the average temperature drops to around 15°C (59°F). Rainfall increases in autumn, with occasional storms and showers, but overall, the weather remains pleasant for outdoor activities.

Winter (December To February)

Winter in Palma is mild compared to many other European destinations. While temperatures can occasionally drop, they generally remain mild. Average temperatures range from 8°C (46°F) in December to 15°C (59°F) in February. Rainfall is relatively higher during this season, and occasional cloudy days are experienced. However, Palma still enjoys a considerable amount of sunshine even in winter.

Precipitation
Palma experiences most of its rainfall during the autumn and winter months, with November and December being the wettest months. However, the overall annual precipitation is relatively low compared to other parts of Spain, averaging around 450-500 millimeters (17-20 inches). The city receives around 60-70 rainy days per year, with short and intense downpours being the typical pattern.

Conclusion
Palma's Mediterranean climate offers visitors a pleasant and enjoyable experience throughout the year. With warm summers, mild winters, and an abundance of sunshine, the city attracts tourists seeking relaxation and outdoor activities. The distinct seasons, moderate rainfall, and comfortable temperatures make Palma an ideal destination for those looking to explore its rich cultural heritage, pristine beaches, and stunning landscapes.

Official Language Of Palma/Other Languages

The official language of Palma is Spanish. Spanish, also known as Castilian, is the most widely spoken language in the country, including Palma. However, due to its popularity as a tourist destination, English and other languages are also commonly spoken, particularly in areas frequented by tourists.

Other Spoken Languages

Apart from English and Spanish, there are several other languages spoken in Palma, reflecting the diverse cultural and linguistic backgrounds of its residents and visitors. Some of the languages you may hear in Palma include:

1. Catalan: Catalan is an official language of the Balearic Islands, including Palma. It is widely spoken and used in official and public contexts, alongside Spanish.

2. German: Due to the large number of German tourists and expatriates in Palma, German is also commonly spoken, especially in tourist areas and among the local German community.

3. Italian: Italian is another language that you may encounter in Palma, as Italy is a significant source of tourism and there are Italian residents living in the city.

4. French: French is spoken by both tourists and residents in Palma, as it is a popular language worldwide and France is a significant source of tourism for the Balearic Islands.

5. Dutch: Dutch tourists and expatriates contribute to the presence of Dutch in Palma, particularly in areas popular among Dutch visitors.

It's important to note that while English and Spanish are the most widely spoken languages in Palma, especially in the tourism industry, the city is a multicultural and multilingual hub, where you may come across other languages spoken by various communities and visitors.

Palma's Official Currency

The official currency of Palma is the Euro (€). Palma is the capital city of the Balearic Islands in Spain, and like the rest of Spain, it uses the Euro as its official currency. The Euro is also the official currency of many other European Union member countries. Banknotes and coins denominated in Euros are used for transactions in Palma and throughout Spain.

System Of Government In Palma

Palma is the capital city of the Balearic Islands in Spain. The Balearic Islands, including Palma, are part of the autonomous community of the Balearic Islands, which has its own system of government within the framework of the Spanish government.

At the regional level, the Balearic Islands have a parliamentary system of government. The executive branch is headed by a President, who is elected by the regional parliament, known as the Parliament of the Balearic Islands. The President appoints members of the government, known as the Council of Government, from among the parliament members. The Council of Government is responsible for the day-to-day administration and implementation of regional policies.

The Parliament of the Balearic Islands is a unicameral legislature, meaning it consists of a single chamber. The members of the parliament, known as deputies, are elected through a proportional representation system. The parliament is responsible for enacting regional laws, approving the regional budget, and overseeing the actions of the government.

It's important to note that political structures and systems of government can evolve over time, so it's advisable to refer to up-to-date sources or official government websites to obtain the most current information on the system of government in Palma and the Balearic Islands.

Brief History Of Palma

Palma, also known as Palma de Mallorca, has a rich history that dates back to ancient times. Here is a brief overview of the history of Palma:

1. Ancient Times: The area around Palma has been inhabited since prehistoric times, with evidence of human presence dating back to at least 6000 BCE. The island of Mallorca, where Palma is located, was settled by the Talaiotic culture, which left behind megalithic monuments and structures.

2. Roman Period: In 123 BCE, the Romans conquered Mallorca and established the city of Palmaria Palmensis, which later became known as Palma. The Romans built a flourishing city, complete with a theater, aqueducts, and other public buildings. Palma served as an important port and trading center during this time.

3. Byzantine and Islamic Rule: In the 5th century CE, the Vandals invaded Mallorca, followed by the Byzantine Empire. However, the Byzantines' rule was short-lived, and the island fell under Islamic control in 902 CE. Under Islamic rule, the city experienced a period of prosperity and cultural development.

4. *Christian Reconquest:* In 1229, King James I of Aragon launched a military campaign to retake Mallorca from the Moors. After a brief siege, Palma surrendered to the Christian forces, and the island became part of the Crown of Aragon. The Christian Reconquest led to a decline in Islamic influence and the establishment of Christianity as the dominant religion.

5. *Medieval and Modern Era:* During the Middle Ages, Palma flourished as a trade and maritime hub. It became a coveted target for various European powers, leading to several invasions and occupations. The city faced attacks from pirates and underwent periods of economic instability.

6. *Spanish Civil War and Contemporary Era:* In the 20th century, Palma, like the rest of Spain, experienced political turmoil and the devastating Spanish Civil War (1936-1939). Following the war, under the rule of General Francisco Franco, the country endured a period of political repression and isolation.

7. *Tourism and Modern Development:* In the late 20th century, Palma underwent significant urban development and became a popular tourist destination. The city's historic center was restored, and tourism became a major economic driver for the region. Palma's cultural heritage, picturesque landscapes, and beautiful beaches attracted visitors from around the world.

Today, Palma is a vibrant city that blends its rich history with modern amenities. It continues to be a popular tourist destination, offering a mix of historical sites, stunning architecture, beautiful beaches, and a lively Mediterranean atmosphere.

Why Visit Palma In 2023

There are several reasons why visiting Palma in 2023 can be an excellent choice. Palma, the capital city of the Spanish island of Mallorca, offers a unique blend of history, culture, natural beauty, and vibrant Mediterranean lifestyle. Here are some compelling reasons to visit Palma in 2023:

> *1. Rich Cultural Heritage:* Palma is steeped in history, with a captivating mix of Moorish, Roman, and Gothic architecture. The most famous landmark is La Seu, Palma's stunning Gothic cathedral, which is a must-see attraction. The city's old town, with its narrow cobblestone streets and charming squares, is also a UNESCO World Heritage site.

> *2. Beautiful Beaches:* Palma boasts some of the most breathtaking beaches in the Mediterranean. In 2023, you can enjoy the golden sands and crystal-clear waters of popular

beaches like Playa de Palma, Cala Major, or Illetes. Relax, swim, or indulge in water sports while soaking up the Mediterranean sun.

3. *Gastronomy:* Mallorca's cuisine is a delight for food lovers. In Palma, you can savor traditional Mallorcan dishes, including the famous sobrasada (cured sausage), ensaïmada (sweet pastry), and delicious seafood. The city is also home to numerous top-notch restaurants, many of which offer innovative and creative culinary experiences.

4. *Vibrant Nightlife:* Palma comes alive at night, especially during the summer months. The city offers a vibrant nightlife scene with trendy bars, clubs, and live music venues. Whether you prefer a relaxing drink in a beachfront bar or dancing until dawn in a lively club, Palma has something for everyone.

5. *Cultural Events and Festivals:* Palma hosts various cultural events and festivals throughout the year. In 2023, you might have the opportunity to experience the famous Nit de Foc, a spectacular fireworks display during the Sant Sebastià festival in January, or the lively Festa de l'Etendard, a celebration of Mallorcan history and culture.

6. *Shopping and Fashion:* Palma is a shopper's paradise, offering a wide range of options from high-end boutiques and designer stores to local markets and artisan shops. You can explore the fashionable Passeig des Born, visit the luxurious shops on Avenida Jaume III, or wander through the traditional markets like Mercat de l'Olivar.

7. *Outdoor Activities:* Nature lovers will appreciate the outdoor activities available in and around Palma. From hiking and cycling in the stunning Serra de Tramuntana mountains to water sports such as sailing, kayaking, and windsurfing, there are plenty of options for adventure enthusiasts.

These are just a few reasons why visiting Palma in 2023 can be a fantastic experience. The city's rich history, beautiful beaches, vibrant culture, and lively atmosphere make it an appealing destination for travelers of all interests.

CHAPTER 2

ESSENTIALS FOR YOUR TRIP TO PALMA

Embarking on a journey can be an exciting experience filled with anticipation and adventure. However, inadequate preparation and unforeseen circumstances can quickly turn it into a stressful ordeal.

To help you avoid unnecessary hassles and make your trip truly memorable, this chapter offers valuable insights and practical tips for both novice and seasoned travelers. By following these recommendations, you can ensure a stress-free and seamless travel experience from start to finish.

Ideal Time To Visit Palma

Palma de Mallorca, the stunning capital of the Balearic Islands in Spain, is a destination that attracts travelers from all around the globe. With its captivating blend of history, culture, pristine beaches, and vibrant nightlife, Palma offers a plethora of experiences to suit every visitor's preferences.

However, choosing the ideal time to visit this enchanting city can greatly enhance your overall experience. In this article, we will explore the various factors to consider when planning your trip to Palma and help you find the perfect time to visit.

1. Weather Considerations:

Palma enjoys a Mediterranean climate, characterized by hot summers and mild winters. The weather plays a significant role in determining the best time to visit. From June to September, the city experiences warm temperatures ranging from 25°C to 30°C (77°F to 86°F), making it ideal for sun-seekers and beach enthusiasts. The summer months are also popular due to the abundance of outdoor festivals and events. Spring (April and May) and autumn (October and November) offer milder temperatures, making it pleasant for sightseeing and outdoor activities without the peak season crowds. Winter, from December to February, brings cooler temperatures and occasional rainfall, but it's still a great time to explore Palma's indoor attractions and enjoy the city's festive atmosphere.

2. Tourist Season and Crowds:

Understanding the tourist seasons is crucial for those seeking a balance between favorable weather and avoiding excessive crowds. Palma experiences its peak tourist season during the summer months (June to August) when schools are on vacation and many Europeans head to the island. During this time, the city can get crowded, and prices for accommodation and flights tend to be higher. If you prefer a more relaxed atmosphere, consider visiting in the shoulder seasons of spring (April to May) or autumn (September to October). The city is less crowded, and you can explore the attractions and enjoy the beaches with relative ease.

3. Festivals and Events:
Palma hosts numerous festivals and events throughout the year, adding an extra layer of cultural richness to your visit. One of the most significant celebrations is the Sant Joan festival in late June, featuring bonfires, fireworks, and lively street parties. If you're interested in contemporary art, consider visiting during the Nit de l'Art in September, when galleries and museums open their doors late into the night. The Christmas season (December) brings festive markets, concerts, and captivating decorations, creating a magical ambiance in the city.

4. Outdoor Activities:
If you plan to engage in outdoor activities, such as swimming, sunbathing, or water sports, the summer months are the ideal time to visit Palma. The beaches are at their finest, and the warm sea temperature invites you to take a refreshing dip. Spring and autumn offer pleasant temperatures for activities like hiking, cycling,

and exploring the city's charming streets and parks. Winter, although cooler, is still suitable for outdoor excursions if you're prepared for milder temperatures and occasional rainfall.

5. Budget Considerations:
Traveling during the off-peak season can help you save money on accommodation, flights, and tourist activities. Palma tends to be more affordable from November to February, excluding the Christmas and New Year period. Prices for flights and hotels can rise during the summer months and during major festivals, so consider planning your visit during the shoulder seasons for better deals.

Determining the ideal time to visit Palma requires careful consideration of weather preferences, tourist seasons, festivals, outdoor activities, and budget constraints. Whether you're seeking a vibrant summer vacation or a peaceful off-season retreat, Palma offers something for everyone. Plan accordingly, and you're sure to have an unforgettable experience exploring the beauty and charm of this captivating Mediterranean city.

Visas And Documents Requirements (If Visiting From Outside Spain)

Palma, the vibrant capital city of the Balearic Islands in Spain, attracts millions of tourists every year with its stunning beaches, historic sites, and lively atmosphere. If you're planning a trip to Palma, it's essential to understand the visa requirements to ensure a smooth and hassle-free journey. This article provides a detailed overview of the visa regulations for traveling to Palma, including information on visa-exempt countries, Schengen visas, and essential documents for entry.

1. Visa-Exempt Countries:

The first thing to determine is whether you require a visa to enter Palma. Spain is a member of the Schengen Area, a group of 26 European countries that have abolished internal border controls. As a result, citizens of certain countries can visit Palma and other Schengen countries for tourism or business purposes without a visa for a limited period. Some common visa-exempt countries include the United States, Canada, Australia, New Zealand, Japan, South Korea, and most European Union (EU) member states.

2. Schengen Visas:

If you are not a citizen of a visa-exempt country, you will need to obtain a Schengen visa to visit

Palma. A Schengen visa allows you to enter and travel within the Schengen Area, including Spain. The visa application process typically involves submitting various documents, such as a completed application form, passport-sized photos, a valid passport, travel insurance, proof of accommodation, proof of financial means, and a detailed travel itinerary.

Types of Schengen Visas:
There are several types of Schengen visas, including:

a. Uniform Schengen Visa (USV): This visa allows for short stays of up to 90 days within a 180-day period. It is suitable for tourists and individuals traveling for business purposes.

b. Limited Territorial Validity Visa (LTV): This visa restricts travel to specific Schengen countries and is suitable for those with compelling reasons to visit only a certain area, excluding others.

c. National Visas: If you plan to stay in Palma or any other part of Spain for more than 90 days, you will need to apply for a national visa. These visas require additional documentation and have specific requirements based on the purpose of your stay, such as study, work, or family reunification.

Applying for a Schengen Visa

To apply for a Schengen visa, you will generally need to visit the Spanish consulate or embassy in your home country. The application process may vary slightly depending on your location, so it is advisable to consult the consulate's official website or contact them directly for accurate and up-to-date information. Ensure that you allow sufficient time for the visa processing, as it can take several weeks.

Essential Documents:

When applying for a Schengen visa, you will typically be required to provide the following essential documents:

a. Valid passport: Ensure that your passport remains valid for at least three months beyond your intended departure date from the Schengen Area.

b. Application form: Fill out the visa application form accurately and completely.

c. Passport-sized photos: Provide recent photographs that meet the specifications outlined by the consulate or embassy.

d. Travel itinerary: Include details of your flights, accommodation, and planned activities in Palma.

e. Travel insurance: Obtain comprehensive travel insurance that covers medical emergencies and repatriation for the duration of your stay.

f. Proof of accommodation: Provide hotel reservations or a letter of invitation from a host in Palma, depending on your travel plans.

g. Proof of financial means: Show evidence of sufficient funds to cover your stay in Palma, such as bank statements or sponsorship letters.

Other Visa Options

Besides the Schengen visa, there are a few other visa options that may be applicable depending on your specific circumstances. These include:

1. Work Visa: If you plan to work in Palma, you will need to apply for a work visa. This type of visa is typically obtained through a sponsoring employer in Palma who must provide documentation to support your employment. The requirements and application process for work visas can vary depending on the specific job and your qualifications.

2. *Student Visa:* If you are planning to study in Palma for a period longer than 90 days, you will need to apply for a student visa. This visa is issued to individuals who have been accepted into a recognized educational institution in Palma and can provide proof of enrollment and financial means to support their studies.

3. *Family Reunification Visa:* If you have family members who are residents or citizens of Palma, you may be eligible for a family reunification visa. This visa allows you to join your family members in Palma for an extended period. The requirements and process for family reunification visas can vary, so it's best to consult the Spanish consulate or embassy for detailed information.

4. *Entrepreneur Visa:* Palma offers specific visa programs for entrepreneurs and investors who wish to establish or invest in businesses in the region. These programs usually have specific criteria, such as a minimum investment amount, job creation requirements, and a business plan. If you meet the eligibility criteria, you can apply for an entrepreneur or investor visa.

It's important to note that the requirements and application processes for these visa options can vary, and it's advisable to consult the Spanish consulate or embassy in your home country for the most accurate and up-to-date information. They will be able to guide you through the specific requirements and procedures based on your circumstances.

What To Pack For Your Trip To Palma

To ensure a smooth and enjoyable trip, it's essential to pack wisely. This article will provide a detailed guide on what to pack for your trip to Palma, considering the climate, activities, and local customs.

Clothing

> **Lightweight and breathable clothing:** Palma enjoys a Mediterranean climate with hot summers, so pack lightweight and breathable clothes like shorts, skirts, dresses, and t-shirts.

> **Swimwear:** Don't forget to pack your swimsuit to make the most of the pristine beaches and crystal-clear waters.

Comfortable walking shoes: Palma is a city best explored on foot, so bring comfortable walking shoes or sandals.

Light jacket or sweater: Although Palma has warm temperatures, evenings can get cooler, especially during spring and autumn, so bring a light jacket or sweater.

Essentials And Accessories

Sun protection: Pack sunscreen with a high SPF, sunglasses, a wide-brimmed hat, and a beach umbrella to shield yourself from the sun's rays.

Travel adapter: Remember to pack a universal travel adapter to charge your electronic devices.

Backpack or day bag: A small backpack or day bag will come in handy for carrying essentials while exploring the city or embarking on day trips.

Travel documents: Bring your passport, identification, travel insurance, flight tickets, and any necessary visas or permits.

Cash and cards: Have some local currency (Euros) and international credit or debit cards for convenience.

Mobile phone and charger: Don't forget your mobile phone and charger to stay connected and capture memorable moments.

Toiletries And Medications

Personal hygiene products: Pack travel-sized toiletries, including toothpaste, toothbrush, shampoo, conditioner, soap, and any other personal care items you may need.

Medications: If you take prescription medications, ensure you have an adequate supply for the duration of your trip. Additionally, consider carrying over-the-counter medications for common ailments like headaches or allergies.

Entertainment And Gadgets

E-reader or books: If you enjoy reading, pack an e-reader or a few books to keep yourself entertained during downtime.

Camera or smartphone: Palma's picturesque landscapes and architectural marvels warrant capturing, so bring a camera or ensure your smartphone has a good camera.

Travel guides and maps: Consider bringing this travel guide and a map to help you navigate the city and discover its hidden gems.

Miscellaneous

Reusable water bottle: Stay hydrated by carrying a reusable water bottle that you can refill throughout the day.

Travel umbrella: While Palma enjoys plenty of sunny days, it's wise to pack a small travel umbrella in case of unexpected showers.

Beach towel or mat: If you plan to spend time at the beach, bring a lightweight beach towel or mat for relaxation.

Snacks and water: If you have specific dietary preferences or plan for long excursions, pack some snacks and water to keep you fueled.

Packing appropriately for your trip to Palma is crucial for a comfortable and enjoyable experience. By following this comprehensive guide, you'll ensure you have the essential items needed for exploring the city, enjoying the beaches, and embracing the local culture. Remember to pack light and focus on the essentials, allowing you to make the most of your unforgettable trip to Palma.

Getting To Palma

From Within Mallorca (The Island)

When traveling from within the island of Mallorca to Palma, the capital city, you have several transportation options to choose from. Here are the most common methods of getting to Palma:

1. Bus: Mallorca has an extensive bus network that connects different towns and villages to Palma. The Empresa Municipal de Transports (EMT) operates buses within Palma, while the Consorci de Transports de Mallorca (CTM) runs intercity buses. You can check the bus schedules and routes on their respective websites or at the bus stations.

2. Train: The Train de l'Est, also known as the Ferrocarril de Sóller, is a scenic narrow-gauge railway that connects Palma to the picturesque town of Sóller. The train journey offers stunning views of the island's countryside. Once you reach Sóller, you can transfer to a bus or take a tram to Palma.

3. Car: If you have access to a car, driving to Palma is relatively straightforward. Mallorca has a well-maintained road network, and the journey from most locations on the island to Palma is convenient. However, traffic and parking can be challenging in the city center, so it's advisable to plan your parking arrangements in advance.

4. Taxi: Taxis are widely available in Mallorca, and you can easily find one to take you to Palma. Taxis operate on meters, and the fares are regulated. Make sure to confirm the approximate cost with the driver before starting your journey.

5. Bicycle: Mallorca is known for its cycling routes, and if you enjoy cycling, you can ride a bike to Palma. The island has dedicated cycling paths and scenic coastal roads. Some areas provide bike rental services, making it convenient to explore Mallorca on two wheels.

These transportation options provide various choices depending on your preferences, budget, and the distance you need to travel within the island. Consider factors such as travel time, cost, and convenience when selecting the most suitable option for your journey to Palma.

From Outside The Island

If you are traveling to Palma from outside the island of Mallorca, the primary means of transportation are by air or by sea. Here are the options available:

1. By Air: The island is served by Palma de Mallorca Airport (PMI), which is the third-largest airport in Spain and offers both domestic and international flights. Many major airlines operate regular flights to Palma from various cities in Europe and other parts of the world. Once you arrive at the airport, you can take a taxi, bus, or arrange for private transportation to reach Palma city center.

2. By Sea: If you prefer a more scenic and leisurely option, you can travel to Palma by sea. Palma has a well-equipped port that accommodates cruise ships and ferries. Several ferry companies operate routes connecting Palma to mainland Spain and other Mediterranean destinations. The most common routes are from Barcelona, Valencia, and Ibiza. The duration of the journey will vary depending on the origin and type of vessel.

If you prefer to travel to Palma from outside the island of Mallorca by your personal vehicle, you have the option to bring your car or motorcycle on a ferry.

Several ferry companies operate routes between mainland Spain and Mallorca, allowing you to bring your vehicle along. The most common departure ports on the Spanish mainland are Barcelona, Valencia, and Denia. The journey durations can vary depending on the departure port and the type of ferry, ranging from around 5 to 8 hours. Once you arrive in the port of Palma, you can drive your vehicle to the city center or any other destination on the island.

When planning your trip by personal vehicle, it's important to consider the ferry schedules, availability, and book your tickets in advance, especially during peak travel seasons. Also, remember to check if there are any specific regulations or requirements for bringing your vehicle on board the ferry.

Once you arrive in Palma, you can use your personal vehicle to explore the city and travel around the island at your convenience. Mallorca has a well-maintained road network, and driving can be a convenient way to access various attractions and destinations on the island. Just keep in mind that traffic and parking can be challenging in busy areas, so plan accordingly and familiarize yourself with parking options in Palma.

It's worth noting that flight and ferry schedules may vary depending on the season, so it's advisable to check the current availability and timings when planning your trip.

Getting Around Palma

To get around Palma, the capital city of the Spanish island of Mallorca, you have several transportation options available. Here are some ways to navigate the city:

1. Walking: Palma's city center is compact and pedestrian-friendly, making it easy to explore on foot. Many of the main attractions, shops, and restaurants are within walking distance of each other.

2. Bicycles: Palma has a bike-sharing program called Bicipalma, which provides bicycles for rent. You can find Bicipalma stations throughout the city where you can pick up and drop off bikes. Cycling is a popular way to get around, especially along the city's beach promenade.

3. Public Transportation: Palma has an extensive public transportation network, including buses and trains, operated by Empresa Municipal de Transportes (EMT). Buses are the most common mode of public transportation and cover various routes within the city and surrounding areas. You can purchase tickets onboard or at EMT kiosks. The train service connects Palma with other towns on the island.

4. *Taxis:* Taxis are readily available in Palma, and you can find taxi stands at major transportation hubs, tourist areas, and throughout the city. Taxis are metered, and you can hail them on the street or call a taxi company to book a ride.

5. *Car Rental:* If you prefer the flexibility of having your own vehicle, you can rent a car in Palma. There are several car rental companies in the city, including international brands. Keep in mind that parking in the city center can be challenging, and some areas may have restricted access.

6. *Hop-on Hop-off Bus:* Palma also offers a hop-on hop-off tourist bus service, which allows you to explore the city's main attractions at your own pace. These buses typically follow a predefined route, and you can get on and off at designated stops.

7. *Ride Sharing Services:* There are ride-hailing services that operate in the city. The most popular local ride-hailing app in Palma is called "Free Now" (formerly known as MyTaxi). Free Now allows you to book a taxi through the app and offers similar features to Uber and Lyft, including upfront pricing and cashless payments. It's a convenient option if you prefer the convenience of booking a taxi using your smartphone.

To use Free Now or any other ride-hailing service in Palma, you will need to download the respective app, create an account, and provide your payment information. Once you have the app installed, you can request a ride, track your driver's location, and pay for the trip within the app.

Keep in mind that while ride-hailing services provide a convenient and reliable way to get around, fares may vary depending on demand and time of day. Additionally, during busy periods, such as major events or holidays, availability may be limited, so it's a good idea to plan ahead or consider alternative transportation options if necessary.

It's important to note that Palma can get busy during peak tourist seasons, so it's advisable to plan your transportation accordingly and allow for some extra time when moving around the city.

Accommodations In Palma (Where To Stay In Palma)

When it comes to accommodations in Palma, there are several options available to suit different preferences and budgets. Here are some suggestions for each category you mentioned:

Hotels And Resorts

Here are the best hotels and resorts in Palma, Mallorca, along with a brief description of each:

> **1. Belmond La Residencia:** A luxurious hotel nestled in the charming village of Deià, offering breathtaking views of the Tramuntana Mountains and the Mediterranean Sea. It features elegant rooms, world-class amenities, a spa, multiple dining options, and an art gallery.

> **2. Hotel Hospes Maricel & Spa:** Located on the seafront in Illetas, this 5-star hotel combines contemporary design with historic charm. It offers stylish rooms, a spa with indoor and outdoor pools, direct access to the sea, and a renowned restaurant serving Mediterranean cuisine.

> **3. Sant Francesc Hotel Singular:** Housed in a restored 19th-century mansion in the heart of Palma's Old Town, this boutique hotel offers a blend of traditional architecture and modern elegance. It features beautifully designed rooms, a rooftop pool, a spa, and a restaurant serving Mediterranean gastronomy.

4. Can Cera Hotel: Situated in a renovated 17th-century palace in Palma's historic center, Can Cera Hotel offers a luxurious stay with spacious rooms, an intimate courtyard, a rooftop terrace, a wellness area, and a gourmet restaurant serving Mallorcan cuisine.

5. Hotel Convent de la Missió: Set in a former 17th-century convent in Palma's old town, this boutique hotel combines contemporary design with historic elements. It features stylish rooms, a spa, an outdoor pool, a gastronomic restaurant, and an art gallery.

6. Castillo Hotel Son Vida: Perched on a hilltop overlooking Palma Bay, this iconic castle hotel offers opulent accommodations, stunning views, golf courses, a spa, multiple restaurants, and a rich history dating back to the 13th century.

7. Nakar Hotel: A modern and chic hotel located in the heart of Palma, close to popular attractions. It features sleek rooms, a rooftop terrace with a pool and panoramic views, a spa, a restaurant, and a rooftop bar.

8. Boutique Hotel Can Alomar: Situated in a renovated 19th-century palace on Palma's exclusive Paseo del Borne, this boutique hotel offers elegant rooms, a rooftop terrace with a pool, a spa, and a restaurant serving Mediterranean cuisine.

9. GPRO Valparaiso Palace & Spa: Located in a tranquil area near the Bellver Castle, this luxury hotel offers spacious rooms, lush gardens, multiple pools, a spa, tennis courts, a fitness center, and panoramic views of Palma Bay.

10. Hotel Cort: Situated in the heart of Palma's La Lonja district, this boutique hotel offers stylish rooms, a rooftop terrace, a restaurant specializing in Mediterranean cuisine, and a vibrant atmosphere close to the city's best nightlife spots.

Bed And Breakfasts

Here are some of the best bed and breakfasts in Palma, Mallorca:

1. Ca'n Savella: Located in Palma's Old Town, this charming bed and breakfast offers comfortable rooms with traditional Mallorcan decor. It provides a cozy and personalized atmosphere, delicious breakfast, and a central location close to attractions and restaurants.

2. Hotel Tres: Although primarily a boutique hotel, Hotel Tres in Palma also offers bed and breakfast options. It features stylish rooms, a rooftop terrace with panoramic views, a courtyard, and a breakfast buffet with a variety of options.

3. *Posada Terra Santa:* Situated in a restored 16th-century mansion in Palma's historic center, this boutique hotel offers a bed and breakfast experience with elegant rooms, a rooftop terrace, a spa, and a delicious breakfast served in a beautiful courtyard.

4. *Ca Sa Padrina:* Located in the charming Santa Catalina neighborhood, this cozy bed and breakfast offers comfortable rooms with a Mallorcan touch. It provides a friendly atmosphere, a lovely garden, and a delicious breakfast with homemade pastries.

5. *Casa Del Monte:* Turismo de Interior: This bed and breakfast is located in a historic building in the heart of Palma's old town. It offers individually decorated rooms, a peaceful courtyard, and a delightful breakfast served in a cozy dining area.

6. *Can Bordoy Grand House & Garden:* This luxury boutique hotel offers a bed and breakfast experience in a beautifully restored 16th-century mansion. It features luxurious rooms, a tranquil garden, a rooftop terrace, and a delightful breakfast served in a charming setting.

7. *Boutique Hotel Calatrava:* Located in the historic Calatrava neighborhood, this boutique hotel offers comfortable rooms, a rooftop terrace with stunning views, and a delicious breakfast served in a cozy dining area. It provides a peaceful retreat in the heart of Palma.

8. *Palau Sa Font:* Situated in a 16th-century palace in Palma's Old Town, this bed and breakfast offers elegant rooms, a charming courtyard, and a breakfast buffet with a selection of local and international dishes. It provides a blend of historic charm and modern comfort.

9. *Can Blau Homes Adults Only:* This adults-only bed and breakfast is located in a traditional Mallorcan townhouse in Palma's Santa Catalina neighborhood. It offers stylish rooms, a communal lounge area, and a tasty breakfast served in a cozy atmosphere.

10. *La Mimosa Guesthouse:* Nestled in the charming neighborhood of El Terreno, this guesthouse offers comfortable rooms with a cozy and welcoming atmosphere. It features a lovely garden, a communal kitchen, and a breakfast buffet with homemade specialties.

Please note that the availability and offerings of bed and breakfast establishments may vary over time. It's recommended to check their websites or contact them directly for the most up-to-date information.

Vacation Rentals And Apartments

For for this option, here are some vacation rentals and apartment options in Palma, Mallorca:

> **1. Airbnb:** Airbnb offers a wide range of vacation rentals and apartments in Palma, allowing you to choose from various locations, sizes, and amenities. You can find apartments in the city center, near the beach, or in residential areas, catering to different budgets and preferences.

> **2. HomeAway:** HomeAway is another popular platform for finding vacation rentals and apartments in Palma. It provides a variety of options, including apartments with sea views, villas with private pools, and cozy townhouses in different neighborhoods of Palma.

> **3. Booking.com:** Booking.com also offers a selection of vacation rentals and apartments in Palma. You can filter your search based on location, facilities, and guest reviews to find the perfect accommodation for your stay.

> **4. VRBO:** VRBO (Vacation Rentals By Owner) is a platform that specializes in vacation rentals, including apartments, villas, and houses. It offers

a range of options in Palma, allowing you to book directly with the property owner.

5. Wimdu: Wimdu is a platform that connects travelers with local hosts offering vacation rentals and apartments. You can find a variety of options in Palma, whether you're looking for a cozy apartment in the city or a beachfront villa.

When booking vacation rentals or apartments, it's important to carefully review the property details, read guest reviews, and communicate with the host to ensure the accommodation meets your needs and preferences.

Budget And Hostel Options

Here are some budget and hostel options in Palma, Mallorca:

1. Hostal Pons: Located in the heart of Palma's historic center, Hostal Pons offers affordable accommodation with comfortable rooms and a friendly atmosphere. It's within walking distance of major attractions and provides easy access to public transportation.

2. Hostal Apuntadores: Situated in the lively La Lonja neighborhood, Hostal Apuntadores is a budget-friendly option offering basic yet clean and comfortable rooms. It's surrounded by restaurants, bars, and shops, and it's just a short walk from Palma Cathedral and the waterfront.

3. Hostal Regina: This family-run guest house is located in Palma's Old Town, close to Plaza Mayor and the city's main shopping areas. Hostal Regina provides budget-friendly rooms with shared bathrooms and a communal kitchen area.

4. Hostal Terramar: Situated near the Portixol area and the beach, Hostal Terramar offers affordable rooms with a relaxed and friendly atmosphere. It's a good option for those looking for budget accommodation with proximity to the sea.

5. Albergue Juvenil Palma: This youth hostel is ideal for budget travelers and backpackers. Located in the Marivent area, it offers dormitory-style rooms, a communal kitchen, and a social lounge. It's a short walk from Cala Mayor beach and well-connected to the city center by public transportation.

6. Hostel Fleming: Located in a residential area of Palma, Hostel Fleming offers affordable accommodation with a communal kitchen, shared bathrooms, and a cozy common area. It's a good option for budget-conscious travelers seeking a quiet and comfortable stay.

7. Hostal Tierramar: Located in the Can Pastilla area, Hostal Tierramar offers affordable rooms just a short walk from the beach. It provides simple yet comfortable accommodations, a communal kitchen, and a friendly atmosphere.

8. Hostel Urban Sea Atocha 113: Situated in the trendy Santa Catalina neighborhood, this hostel offers budget-friendly dormitory-style rooms with shared bathrooms. It features a rooftop terrace, a communal kitchen, and a social lounge area.

9. Hostel Fleming Capdepera: Located in the Capdepera area, this hostel offers affordable accommodation with shared facilities. It provides basic rooms, a communal kitchen, and a relaxed environment for budget-conscious travelers.

10. Hostal Bonany: Situated near the Plaza de España, Hostal Bonany offers budget-friendly rooms in a central location. It provides simple and clean accommodations, and it's within walking distance of major attractions and public transportation.

Please note that availability and prices may vary, so it's recommended to check with each accommodation directly or through booking platforms for the most up-to-date information.

Unique Stays And Luxury Retreats

Here are some unique stays and luxury retreats in Palma, Mallorca:

1. Castell Son Claret: Located in the stunning countryside near Palma, this luxury retreat is set within a historic castle surrounded by lush gardens and vineyards. It offers luxurious rooms, a spa, gourmet dining, and a peaceful atmosphere.

2. Gran Hotel Son Net: Situated in the countryside near the village of Puigpunyent, this luxurious hotel occupies a restored 17th-century mansion. It features elegant rooms, a spa, an outdoor pool, and panoramic views of the Tramuntana Mountains.

3. Sa Pedrissa: Nestled on a hillside overlooking the Mediterranean Sea, this boutique hotel offers a unique and intimate stay in a 17th-century manor house. It provides luxurious rooms, a pool, a restaurant, and breathtaking views of the coast.

4. Finca Serena: Located in the rural countryside near Montuïri, Finca Serena is a luxurious retreat set on a vast estate. It offers stylish rooms, a spa, an outdoor pool, a farm-to-table restaurant, and serene surroundings perfect for relaxation.

5. Can Simoneta Hotel: Perched on a cliffside near the town of Canyamel, this adults-only hotel offers stunning views of the sea and direct access to a private beach. It features luxurious rooms, a spa, multiple pools, and a restaurant serving Mediterranean cuisine.

6. Son Brull Hotel & Spa: Situated in the tranquil countryside near Pollença, Son Brull Hotel & Spa is a luxury retreat set within a former monastery. It offers stylish rooms, a spa, a Michelin-starred restaurant, and beautiful grounds with olive groves and vineyards.

7. Cap Rocat: Located in a former military fortress overlooking the Bay of Palma, Cap Rocat offers a truly unique and exclusive stay. It features luxurious rooms, private plunge pools, a spa, a saltwater pool, and direct access to a secluded beach.

Please note that availability and offerings may vary, so it's advisable to check with each establishment directly or through booking platforms for the most up-to-date information on unique stays and luxury retreats in Palma.

CHAPTER 3

THINGS TO DO IN PALMA

In this chapter, we will uncover the captivating wonders of Palma, a vibrant city located on the stunning island of Mallorca. From basking in the Mediterranean sun on pristine beaches to immersing oneself in rich history and culture, Palma offers a diverse range of experiences for every visitor.

What Should You Do in Palma?

From nature lovers to outdoor enthusiasts, art lovers to history buffs, Palma has something to offer for every type of traveler. Here, we will explore a variety of activities and attractions based on your interests, so you can plan the perfect itinerary for your trip to Palma.

Must See Landmarks

Sure! Here are some top attractions in Palma, Mallorca you could explore:

> ***La Seu Cathedral***: A stunning Gothic cathedral located in the heart of Palma. It's one of the city's most iconic landmarks and offers breathtaking views from its rooftop terrace.

Bellver Castle: A unique circular castle situated on a hill overlooking the city. It houses a historical museum and provides panoramic views of Palma and the surrounding area.

Palma Old Town: Explore the charming narrow streets of the historic center, where you'll find beautiful architecture, quaint squares, and impressive buildings like the Lonja de Palma (Old Fish Market).

Royal Palace of La Almudaina: Located next to the Cathedral, this historic palace dates back to the Moorish period and later became a royal residence. Visitors can explore its stunning interiors, including the throne room and royal apartments.

Plaça Major: The main square of Palma, Plaça Major is a vibrant hub of activity. It features colorful facades, outdoor cafes, and a lively atmosphere. It's a great place to relax, people-watch, and soak in the local ambiance.

Passeig des Born: A picturesque tree-lined avenue, Passeig des Born is a popular promenade in the heart of Palma. It's lined with elegant buildings, luxury shops, and cafes. The avenue leads to Parc de la Mar and offers stunning views of the Cathedral.

Es Baluard de Sant Pere: This impressive bastion is part of the city walls of Palma. It offers panoramic views of the city's harbor and is a perfect spot for a leisurely walk or to capture some beautiful photographs.

Lonja de Palma de Mallorca: Also known as the Old Fish Market, Lonja de Palma is a Gothic-style building dating back to the 15th century. It features intricate stonework and impressive architecture. Today, it serves as an exhibition space and cultural center.

Arab Baths (Banys Àrabs): Tucked away in the narrow streets of Palma's old town, these 10th-century Arab baths are a hidden gem. The well-preserved baths offer a glimpse into the city's Moorish past and are an oasis of tranquility.

These landmarks showcase the rich history and architectural beauty of Palma. Exploring these sites will give you a deeper understanding of the city's cultural heritage.

Iconic Museums And Galleries

Es Baluard Museum of Modern and Contemporary Art: This museum showcases a diverse collection of Balearic and Spanish art from the 20th and 21st centuries, including works by renowned artists.

Joan Miró Foundation: Dedicated to the life and work of the famous Catalan artist Joan Miró, this museum features a wide range of his paintings, sculptures, and other artistic creations.

Palau March Museum: Located in a former mansion, this museum houses an extensive collection of sculptures, ceramics, and medieval art. It also offers beautiful views of Palma Bay.

CaixaForum Palma: Located in a beautifully restored 19th-century building, CaixaForum Palma is an art center that hosts rotating exhibitions, cultural events, and educational programs. It showcases a diverse range of contemporary art and cultural exhibitions.

Can Prunera Modernist Museum: Situated in the charming town of Sóller, a short distance from Palma, Can Prunera is a stunning modernist mansion turned museum. It features an impressive collection of modernist art, including works by renowned artists such as Picasso and Miró.

Es Llonja: This contemporary art center is dedicated to promoting contemporary art and supporting local artists. It hosts exhibitions, workshops, and cultural events, showcasing a range of artistic disciplines and perspectives.

Natural Wonders And Parks

Though some of these sites are not inside Palma, they are just a few minutes drive from Palma should you consider taking a day trip away from Palma.

Parc de la Mar: A scenic waterfront park situated next to the cathedral, with a large reflecting pool and lush greenery. It's a great spot to relax and enjoy the views of the cathedral and the sea.

Serra de Tramuntana: This mountain range, designated as a UNESCO World Heritage Site, offers breathtaking natural beauty. Explore its hiking trails, picturesque villages, and enjoy panoramic vistas.

Palma Beaches: Palma is blessed with several stunning beaches where you can soak up the sun and enjoy the crystal-clear waters of the Mediterranean. Some popular beaches include Playa de Palma, Cala Major, and Illetas Beach.

Bellver Forest: Adjacent to Bellver Castle, Bellver Forest is a large wooded area perfect for hiking and nature walks. It offers shady trails, beautiful viewpoints, and a peaceful escape from the city.

Parc Natural de Mondragó: Located in the southeastern part of Mallorca, about an hour's drive from Palma, this natural park is known for its pristine beaches, rugged cliffs, and scenic walking trails. It's a haven for nature lovers and birdwatchers.

Cap de Formentor: Situated on the northeastern tip of Mallorca, Cap de Formentor is a stunning peninsula with dramatic cliffs, turquoise waters, and panoramic views. The drive to the lighthouse offers breathtaking vistas and photo opportunities.

S'Albufera Natural Park: Located near the town of Alcúdia, about 45 minutes from Palma, S'Albufera is a vast wetland reserve and one of the most important bird sanctuaries in the Balearic Islands. It's a paradise for birdwatchers and nature enthusiasts.

These natural wonders and parks allow you to immerse yourself in the island's beauty, whether it's through scenic walks, beach relaxation, or exploring diverse ecosystems. They offer a chance to connect with nature and appreciate Mallorca's natural splendor.

Historic Sites And Architecture

Palau de l'Almudaina: A royal palace originally built as an Arabian fortress, it now serves as the official summer residence of the Spanish Royal Family. You can visit its beautiful rooms and admire the mix of Gothic and Moorish architecture.

Pueblo Español: A recreated Spanish village showcasing architectural styles from different regions of Spain. It offers a fascinating insight into the country's diverse culture and history.

Can Forteza Rey: A restored 17th-century mansion that now serves as a cultural center. It features impressive architectural details and hosts various exhibitions and events.

Hidden Gems And Local Favorites

Santa Catalina neighborhood: Known for its trendy atmosphere, this neighborhood is filled with cozy cafes, trendy boutiques, and vibrant street art. It's a great place to explore the local food and nightlife scene.

Mercat de l'Olivar: A bustling indoor market where you can find a wide variety of fresh produce, local delicacies, and traditional crafts. It's a great spot to immerse yourself in the local culture and taste some delicious Mallorcan specialties.

Es Jonquet neighborhood: A charming district filled with colorful houses and narrow streets. It offers a glimpse into the traditional fishing village atmosphere of Palma and is a lovely area for a leisurely stroll.

Santa Eulalia Church: Tucked away in the narrow streets of Palma's old town, the Santa Eulalia Church is a hidden gem. It features beautiful Gothic architecture and a tranquil courtyard, providing a peaceful retreat from the bustling city.

Ca'n Joan de S'aigo: This historic cafe and pastry shop is a beloved local institution. It has been serving traditional pastries, hot chocolate, and ice cream since 1700. Don't miss their famous ensaïmadas, a traditional Mallorcan sweet treat.

Mercat de Santa Catalina: Located in the trendy Santa Catalina neighborhood, this local market is a vibrant hub of activity. You can find fresh produce, seafood, spices, and local products. It's a great place to immerse yourself in the local food scene and pick up some delicious ingredients.

La Bóveda: Tucked away in a hidden corner of Palma's old town, La Bóveda is a traditional tapas bar loved by locals. It offers a cozy atmosphere and serves a wide variety of delicious tapas, including local specialties like sobrasada and pa amb oli.

Can Joan de S'Aigo: Another popular local spot, Can Joan de S'Aigo is a historic café that has been serving traditional pastries and drinks since 1700. Try their ensaïmadas, hot chocolate, or almond ice cream for a taste of Mallorcan flavors.

Fundación Juan March: This cultural foundation hosts exhibitions, concerts, and other cultural events. It focuses on promoting Spanish and Balearic art and music, offering a unique cultural experience.

Carrer de Sant Miquel: This bustling street in the heart of Palma is a local favorite for shopping and dining. It's lined with boutique shops, cafes, and restaurants, offering a vibrant atmosphere and a chance to explore the local scene.

These hidden gems and local favorites offer a glimpse into the authentic and vibrant side of Palma. They provide opportunities to connect with the local culture, indulge in traditional flavors, and explore lesser-known corners of the city. These are just a few of the many attractions in Palma. The city offers a rich blend of history, culture, and natural beauty, making it a popular destination for visitors.

Whether you are an outdoor enthusiast, a nature lover, art or architecture lover, a foodie, a history buff, a romantic, Palma has everything you need for a wonderful experience.

Other Neighborhoods/Districts Worth Exploring

Here are a few more neighborhoods and districts in Palma, Mallorca, that are worth exploring:

El Terreno: Located west of Palma's city center, El Terreno is a bohemian neighborhood known for its lively nightlife, trendy bars, and clubs. It's a popular area for locals and tourists alike to enjoy a vibrant evening out.

Portixol: Situated east of Palma's city center, Portixol is a charming coastal neighborhood with a picturesque marina and a promenade lined with restaurants and cafes. It's a great place to enjoy a leisurely stroll, relax by the beach, or savor delicious seafood dishes.

La Lonja: Nestled between the Cathedral and the sea, La Lonja is a historic neighborhood characterized by narrow streets, medieval buildings, and charming squares. It's a vibrant area known for its excellent restaurants, trendy bars, and lively atmosphere.

Son Espanyolet: Located west of the city center, Son Espanyolet is a residential neighborhood that offers a quieter and more laid-back atmosphere. It's known for its beautiful traditional Mallorcan houses, local shops, and cozy cafes.

Porta de Sant Antoni: This neighborhood is located just outside the city walls near the Plaza de España. It's a vibrant area with a mix of residential buildings, local shops, and authentic restaurants. It's a great place to experience local life and explore the less touristy side of Palma.

Es Molinar: Situated east of the city center, Es Molinar is a seaside neighborhood that has retained its traditional fishing village charm. It offers a peaceful and relaxed atmosphere, with a lovely beach, waterfront promenade, and excellent seafood restaurants.

These neighborhoods offer a different atmosphere and unique experiences compared to the previously mentioned areas. Exploring these districts will allow you to discover the diverse facets of Palma and delve into the local culture and lifestyle.

Family Friendly Activities In Palma

Here are some family-friendly activities in Palma, Mallorca:

Palma Aquarium: A popular attraction for families, Palma Aquarium offers a fascinating underwater world to explore. You can observe a variety of marine species, walk through tunnels surrounded by sharks, and even have the opportunity to swim with rays.

Katmandu Park: Located in Magaluf, just a short drive from Palma, Katmandu Park is a theme park with a variety of attractions suitable for all ages. It features interactive experiences, 4D cinemas, mini-golf, water slides, and a virtual reality experience.

Western Water Park: Another water park located in Magaluf, Western Water Park is a great place to cool off and have fun. It offers a wide range of water slides, wave pools, lazy rivers, and splash areas suitable for both kids and adults.

Marineland Mallorca: Located in Costa d'en Blanes, Marineland Mallorca combines animal shows with water attractions. You can enjoy dolphin and sea lion shows, as well as watch penguins, reptiles, and tropical fish.

Jungle Parc: Located in Santa Ponsa, Jungle Parc is an adventure park with high ropes courses, zip lines, and obstacles suitable for different age groups. It's a thrilling and active experience for the whole family.

Beaches: Palma has several family-friendly beaches where you can relax, build sandcastles, and enjoy the Mediterranean waters. Some popular options include Playa de Palma, Cala Major, and Illetas Beach.

Palma City Sightseeing Bus: Hop on the open-top sightseeing bus to explore the city at your own pace. The bus takes you to major attractions and allows you to get on and off as you please, making it convenient for families with young children.

Parque de Sa Riera: Located near the city center, Parque de Sa Riera is a park with playgrounds, picnic areas, and open spaces for kids to run and play. It's a great spot for a family outing or a relaxing break from sightseeing.

These family-friendly activities offer a mix of entertainment, education, and outdoor fun. They provide opportunities for kids and adults alike to create lasting memories while exploring the beauty and attractions of Palma, Mallorca.

Day Trips And Excursions From Palma

Palma, the capital city of the Spanish island of Mallorca, offers a great base for exploring the surrounding areas. There are several exciting day trips and excursions you can take from Palma to explore the natural beauty, historic sites, and charming towns of the island. Here are some popular options:

1. Serra de Tramuntana: This UNESCO World Heritage-listed mountain range is located on the northwest coast of Mallorca and offers breathtaking scenery. You can drive or take a guided tour to visit picturesque villages like Valldemossa, Deià, and Sóller, and enjoy hiking or cycling in the stunning landscapes.

2. Formentor Peninsula: Located on the northern tip of Mallorca, the Formentor Peninsula is known for its stunning beaches and rugged cliffs. You can take a scenic drive along the winding roads to Cap de Formentor, visit the lighthouse, and relax on beautiful beaches like Formentor Beach.

3. Cuevas del Drach: These magnificent caves are located on the eastern coast of Mallorca near the town of Porto Cristo. Explore the stunning stalactite formations, take a boat ride on Lake Martel (one of the largest underground lakes in the world), and enjoy a classical music concert inside the caves.

4. *Valldemossa and Port de Sóller:*
Valldemossa, a charming village in the Tramuntana Mountains, is famous for its beautiful architecture and the Royal Carthusian Monastery. After exploring Valldemossa, you can take a vintage wooden train ride from Palma to the picturesque town of Sóller and then hop on a tram to reach the Port de Sóller, known for its sandy beach and scenic harbor.

5. *Palma Nova and Magaluf:* If you're looking for a beach day and some lively entertainment, head to Palma Nova and Magaluf. Located southwest of Palma, these popular resort areas offer beautiful sandy beaches, water sports activities, beachfront bars, restaurants, and vibrant nightlife.

6. *Cabrera Archipelago Maritime-Terrestrial National Park:* Take a boat trip from Palma to the Cabrera Archipelago, a protected national park located south of Mallorca. Explore the pristine beaches, crystal-clear waters, and diverse marine life by snorkeling or scuba diving. The park is also home to an old fortress and a museum showcasing its history.

7. *Alcudia:* Located in the northern part of Mallorca, Alcudia is a charming medieval town with well-preserved walls dating back to the 14th century. Explore the narrow streets, visit the local market (held on Tuesdays and Sundays), and relax on the beautiful sandy beaches nearby.

8. *Cap de Formentor:* In addition to the Formentor Peninsula, you can explore the stunning Cap de Formentor by taking a scenic drive or cycling route. Enjoy panoramic views from various lookout points, such as Mirador Es Colomer, and visit the picturesque beach of Cala Figuera.

9. *Inca:* Known as the "leather town" of Mallorca, Inca is located in the center of the island. It's a great place to shop for leather goods and visit the weekly market held on Thursdays, where you can find local products and traditional crafts.

10. *Caves of Artà:* Located near the town of Artà, these caves offer a fascinating underground adventure. Explore the impressive chambers with stunning stalactite formations, and learn about their geological history during a guided tour.

11. *Wine Tasting in Binissalem:* Mallorca is known for its wine production, and the village of Binissalem, located in the center of the island, is a great place to experience it. Visit local wineries, enjoy wine tastings, and learn about the island's wine-making traditions.

12. Beaches of Es Trenc and Colonia de Sant Jordi: Located in the south of Mallorca, these beautiful beaches offer turquoise waters and long stretches of white sand. Es Trenc is known for its natural beauty and unspoiled coastline, while Colonia de Sant Jordi offers a relaxed beach town atmosphere.

These are just a few examples of the many day trips and excursions you can take from Palma. Whether you're interested in nature, history, or simply relaxing on the beach, Mallorca has plenty to offer beyond its capital city Palma.

Palma's Festivals And Carnivals

Throughout the year, Palma hosts a plethora of lively festivals that showcase its cultural richness and provide a captivating experience for locals and visitors alike. From religious processions to music and dance celebrations, the festivals in Palma offer a glimpse into the city's traditions, history, and spirit. This article delves into some of the most prominent festivals held in Palma, highlighting their significance and the unique experiences they offer.

Annual Cultural Celebrations/Festivals

Sant Sebastià Festival:

One of the most eagerly anticipated festivals in Palma, the Sant Sebastià Festival takes place every January. Honoring the patron saint of the city, it brings together locals and tourists for several days of exuberant celebrations. The festival features a diverse range of activities, including street parades, concerts, firework displays, and traditional dancing. The main event is the "Correfoc," a mesmerizing fire run where costumed demons parade through the streets, accompanied by fireworks and music, creating a spectacular visual spectacle.

Festa de l'Estendard:

In honor of James I, the conqueror of Mallorca, the Festa de l'Estendard (Festival of the Standard) is celebrated annually on December 31st. The festival commences with a colorful parade led by the city's authorities, marching bands, and citizens dressed in medieval attire. The highlight of the festival is the reenactment of the handing over of the city's keys to James I, followed by a solemn mass at the Palma Cathedral. The event captures the medieval history of Palma and pays homage to its cultural heritage.

Nit de Foc:

Translated as the "Night of Fire," Nit de Foc is a remarkable celebration that takes place on the eve of the Feast of St. John, June 23rd. Throughout the city, enormous bonfires are lit, creating a mesmerizing ambiance. Locals gather around the fires, enjoying traditional music, dancing, and feasting on typical Mallorcan delicacies. As midnight approaches, the festivities reach their peak with a magnificent fireworks display illuminating the night sky. Nit de Foc is a joyful and fiery celebration of the summer solstice, where locals come together to welcome the arrival of summer.

Festival de la Mar:
Every summer, Palma's waterfront transforms into a lively stage for the Festival de la Mar (Festival of the Sea). This festival showcases the city's close relationship with the Mediterranean Sea and celebrates its maritime heritage. The event includes various nautical activities, such as regattas, boat races, and sailing competitions. Visitors can explore exhibitions of traditional fishing boats, enjoy live music performances, and indulge in delicious seafood delicacies offered by local vendors. The Festival de la Mar is a perfect blend of entertainment, cultural immersion, and the beauty of Palma's coastal charm.

Festival of the Virgin of Carmen:

Held on July 16th, the Festival of the Virgin of Carmen pays tribute to the patron saint of fishermen and sailors. Palma's fishing community takes center stage during this vibrant celebration, which involves a solemn procession of the Virgin's statue through the streets, followed by a colorful flotilla of decorated boats along the coastline. This festival serves as a reminder of the city's seafaring roots and demonstrates the deep devotion of its people to the Virgin of Carmen.

Music And Art Festivals

Festival de Música de Deià: While not in Palma itself, this renowned music festival takes place in the nearby village of Deià. Held in July and August, it features classical and contemporary music performances by world-class musicians.

Festival Parkalive: Parkalive is an annual music festival held in Parc de la Mar, a beautiful park located near Palma Cathedral. It showcases a variety of music genres, including pop, rock, indie, and electronic music.

Mallorca Live Festival: This multi-genre music festival brings together local and international artists for a weekend of live performances. It usually takes place in May at the Antiguo Aquapark in Calvià, just outside Palma.

Palma's festivals offer a fascinating insight into the city's history, cultural traditions, and vibrant spirit. Whether it's the explosive Correfoc of the Sant Sebastià Festival, the medieval grandeur of the Festa de l'Estendard, the fiery revelry of Nit de Foc, the maritime festivities of the Festival de la Mar, or the religious homage of the Festival of the Virgin of Carmen, each celebration showcases Palma's unique identity. By partaking in these festivals, visitors can immerse themselves in the rich tapestry of Palma's heritage and create unforgettable memories in this captivating city.

Carnival

Carnivals are extravagant celebrations that bring communities together in a burst of color, music, dance, and revelry. Palma embraces the carnival spirit with its own unique flair. These festivities provide locals and tourists with an opportunity to immerse themselves in a joyous atmosphere and experience the vibrant culture of the city. Let's explore the carnivals held in Palma, capturing their essence and highlighting their significance.

1. Carnival de Palma:

The Carnival de Palma is the largest and most popular carnival celebration on the island of Mallorca. It typically takes place in late February or early March, marking the prelude to the Christian season of Lent. The streets of Palma come alive with an explosion of color, as participants don colorful costumes, masks, and elaborate floats. The carnival procession, known as the "Rúas," parades through the city streets, accompanied by energetic music and dancing. Local organizations, groups, and individuals showcase their creativity and enthusiasm, making it a spectacle not to be missed.

2. Sa Rua de Sa Vileta:
Sa Rua de Sa Vileta is a neighborhood-specific carnival celebrated in the Vileta district of Palma. This carnival, held on the Sunday before Ash Wednesday, is known for its strong community participation and traditional elements. Residents of Vileta take pride in crafting their own costumes and floats, showcasing their creativity and neighborhood spirit. The parade winds through the streets, spreading joy and excitement among locals and visitors alike. Sa Rua de Sa Vileta offers an intimate and authentic carnival experience, reflecting the neighborhood's unique identity.

3. Children's Carnival:
In addition to the main carnival events, Palma also hosts a special carnival celebration dedicated to children. The Children's Carnival invites young ones to partake in the festivities, dressing up in their favorite costumes and joining the procession alongside their families. This

event creates a delightful atmosphere filled with laughter, playful activities, and child-friendly entertainment. It allows children to experience the magic of carnival while fostering a sense of community and belonging.

4. Carnival Ball:

The Carnival Ball is a glamorous and elegant affair that adds a touch of sophistication to Palma's carnival celebrations. This formal event takes place in various venues across the city, offering attendees a chance to don their finest attire and enjoy a night of dancing, live music, and entertainment. The Carnival Ball provides a different perspective on the carnival experience, catering to those who appreciate a more refined celebration.

The carnivals in Palma showcase the city's exuberance, creativity, and community spirit. Whether it's the grandeur of the Carnival de Palma, the neighborhood charm of Sa Rua de Sa Vileta, the joy of the Children's Carnival, or the elegance of the Carnival Ball, each celebration contributes to the diverse tapestry of carnival traditions in Palma. Participating in these festivities allows both locals and visitors to embrace the magic of carnival, creating lasting memories and experiencing the vibrant culture of Palma in all its colorful splendor.

Sporting Events

Palma Marathon: The Palma Marathon is held annually in October, attracting runners from around the world. The race starts and finishes in Palma, taking participants through the scenic streets of the city and along the beautiful coastline.

Copa del Rey Regatta: Palma hosts the prestigious Copa del Rey Regatta, one of the most important sailing events in the Mediterranean. Sailors from different countries gather to compete in this week-long regatta held in July or August.

Nightlife In Palma

Palma is renowned for its stunning beaches, historic architecture, and rich cultural heritage. However, when the sun sets, Palma comes alive with an electrifying nightlife scene that rivals some of the best in Europe. From stylish rooftop bars and pulsating nightclubs to cozy taverns and live music venues, Palma offers a diverse range of options to cater to every taste and preference. In this article, we will take an in-depth look at the vibrant and exciting nightlife of Palma, ensuring you make the most of your evenings on this captivating Mediterranean island.

The Historic Center: Lively Streets and Traditional Bars

One of the best ways to experience the nightlife in Palma is by exploring the historic center, where narrow cobblestone streets are filled with bustling bars and taverns. The area around La Lonja and Plaça Major is particularly popular, offering an authentic atmosphere and a wide selection of traditional tapas bars. Visitors can savor local delicacies, indulge in Spanish wines, and immerse themselves in the convivial ambiance that characterizes Palma's traditional nightlife.

Paseo Marítimo: Glamour and Luxury

Paseo Marítimo, the city's stunning waterfront promenade, transforms into a glamorous hub of nightlife after dark. This area is home to some of Palma's most exclusive and sophisticated venues, including chic cocktail bars and high-end nightclubs. Here, you can sip on creative cocktails while enjoying breathtaking views of the marina or dance the night away to the beats of internationally renowned DJs. Paseo Marítimo offers a glitzy and upscale experience, perfect for those seeking a touch of luxury during their nocturnal adventures.

Santa Catalina: Bohemian Vibes and Eclectic Bars

Santa Catalina, a trendy neighborhood just west of the city center, attracts a diverse crowd with its bohemian ambiance and vibrant nightlife. This area is renowned for its eclectic mix of bars, ranging from cozy wine bars to hipster-friendly craft beer joints. Santa Catalina is also famous for its lively street art scene and numerous small music venues hosting local bands and artists. For a laid-back and alternative night out, Santa Catalina provides the perfect setting.

La Llonja: Tapas and Late-Night Socializing

Located near the impressive La Seu Cathedral, the La Llonja district offers a unique blend of history, art, and nightlife. The streets of La Llonja are dotted with stylish cocktail bars, tapas restaurants, and modern lounges. Here, you can savor delicious tapas dishes and mingle with locals and visitors alike, creating a convivial atmosphere that extends well into the late hours of the night. La Llonja is ideal for those looking to socialize, indulge in delectable cuisine, and enjoy a sophisticated yet relaxed evening.

Live Music and Cultural Performances

Palma also boasts a vibrant live music scene, with various venues offering a wide range of musical genres. The Auditorium de Palma, located near the waterfront, hosts classical music concerts, opera performances, and ballet shows. Additionally, numerous bars and clubs feature live bands and DJs playing everything from jazz and blues to rock and electronic music. Whether you prefer intimate jazz clubs or large-scale concert halls, Palma has something to suit all musical tastes.

Palma's nightlife scene is as diverse as the city itself, offering an array of options for nighttime entertainment. From traditional tapas bars and lively streets in the historic center to glamorous waterfront venues and bohemian neighborhoods, Palma ensures a memorable and exciting nightlife experience for all visitors.

CHAPTER 4

DINING IN PALMA

Palma de Mallorca, the stunning capital city of the Spanish island of Mallorca, is renowned for its breathtaking beauty and vibrant culture. While its picturesque landscapes and rich history attract visitors from around the world, Palma is also celebrated for its traditional cuisine that has delighted locals and tourists alike for centuries. The culinary traditions of Palma de Mallorca are deeply rooted in the region's Mediterranean gastronomy, showcasing an abundance of fresh ingredients and a true passion for culinary excellence.

Dining Options

Palma offers a wide range of dining options that cater to various tastes and preferences. From traditional Spanish cuisine to international flavors, there is something for everyone in Palma's vibrant dining scene. In this chapter, we will explore some of the popular dining experiences you can enjoy in Palma.

1. Traditional Spanish Tapas:
No visit to Spain is complete without indulging in tapas, and Palma is no exception. Head to the charming old town, known as La Lonja, where you'll find narrow cobblestone streets lined with

tapas bars and restaurants. Sample an array of small plates, from classic favorites like patatas bravas (spicy potatoes) and jamón ibérico (cured ham) to more adventurous dishes like pulpo a la gallega (Galician-style octopus) and boquerones en vinagre (anchovies in vinegar). Pair your tapas with a glass of local wine or a refreshing sangria for an authentic Spanish dining experience.

2. Seafood Delights:
With its coastal location, Palma is renowned for its fresh seafood. The Santa Catalina neighborhood, just west of the city center, is a hub for seafood restaurants. Feast on mouth watering dishes like paella de mariscos (seafood paella), grilled fish, and seafood platters showcasing the catch of the day. Enjoy the Mediterranean breeze as you savor the flavors of the sea, accompanied by a glass of crisp white wine.

3. Fusion and International Cuisine:
Palma also offers a diverse range of international dining options, blending flavors from around the world. From Asian fusion to Mediterranean-inspired dishes with a contemporary twist, you'll find a variety of culinary delights. Explore the trendy neighborhood of Santa Catalina or the Paseo Marítimo, where you'll discover restaurants

serving innovative dishes crafted by talented chefs. Indulge in sushi, Thai curries, gourmet burgers, or vegetarian/vegan options – the possibilities are endless.

4. Michelin-Starred Experiences:

If you're seeking a truly exceptional dining experience, Palma boasts several Michelin-starred restaurants. These establishments are renowned for their creativity, impeccable service, and exquisite flavors. Treat yourself to a gastronomic journey with tasting menus featuring meticulously crafted dishes made from the finest local and seasonal ingredients. Some of the Michelin-starred restaurants in Palma include Marc Fosh, Adrián Quetglas, and Simply Fosh.

5. Rooftop Dining with Views:

For a memorable dining experience, head to one of Palma's rooftop restaurants and enjoy stunning panoramic views of the city, the harbor, and the Mediterranean Sea. These establishments offer a combination of delectable cuisine and breathtaking scenery. Whether you're enjoying a romantic dinner or a casual meal with friends, the rooftop setting adds a touch of magic to your dining experience.

Palma's dining scene is as diverse as its cultural heritage, offering a culinary adventure for every palate.

From traditional Spanish tapas to international fusion cuisine, seafood delights to Michelin-starred extravaganzas, the city caters to a wide range of tastes and budgets. So, get ready to savor the flavors of Palma as you embark on a delightful culinary journey through the city's vibrant dining scene.

Palma's Cuisines

When it comes to traditional cuisine in Palma, Mallorca, there are several dishes that showcase the region's culinary heritage and local flavors. Here is a list of traditional Palma cuisines that you should try when visiting the city:

> *Sobrasada:* This cured sausage is a Mallorcan specialty made from ground pork, paprika, salt, and other spices. It has a rich, smoky flavor and a soft, spreadable texture. Sobrasada is often enjoyed on crusty bread or incorporated into various recipes.

> *Ensaimada:* Perhaps one of the most iconic pastries in Mallorca, the ensaimada is a sweet, spiral-shaped pastry made with flour, sugar, eggs, and pork lard. It has a light, fluffy texture and is typically dusted with powdered sugar. Ensaimadas can be enjoyed plain or filled with cream, custard, or other sweet fillings.

Pa amb oli: This simple yet delicious dish is a staple in Mallorcan cuisine. It consists of rustic bread rubbed with ripe tomatoes, garlic, olive oil, and a sprinkle of salt. It is often served with cured meats, cheese, or olives, and makes for a satisfying snack or light meal.

Tumbet: Tumbet is a hearty vegetable dish that features layers of sliced potatoes, eggplant, and red bell peppers, typically fried and then baked in a tomato sauce. It is often served as a side dish or a vegetarian main course and is a popular choice for locals and visitors alike.

Frito Mallorquín: Frito Mallorquín is a traditional meat dish that showcases the island's agricultural heritage. It consists of tender pieces of lamb or pork, sautéed with potatoes, bell peppers, garlic, and herbs. The dish is rich in flavors and is a comforting, hearty option for meat lovers.

Caldereta de Langosta: This is a luxurious lobster stew that highlights the island's abundant seafood. The dish features succulent chunks of lobster cooked in a flavorful broth with tomatoes, onions, garlic, and spices. It is a true delicacy and often served on special occasions or at seafood restaurants along the coast.

Sopas Mallorquinas: Sopas Mallorquinas, also known as Mallorcan soups, are a rustic and hearty dish made with day-old bread, broth, vegetables (such as tomatoes, onions, and peppers), and meat (such as lamb or pork). The bread soaks up the flavors, creating a comforting and filling soup.

Crespells: Crespells are traditional Mallorcan cookies that are typically enjoyed during festivals and holidays. They are made with flour, sugar, eggs, lard, and a hint of anise or lemon zest. The cookies come in various shapes, such as flowers or stars, and are often decorated with powdered sugar.

Arros Brut: Arros Brut, which translates to "dirty rice," is a hearty and flavorsome rice dish that showcases the influence of Mallorca's agricultural roots. It typically consists of rice cooked with a variety of meats such as pork, rabbit, and chicken, along with vegetables, herbs, and spices. The combination of meats and aromatic flavors makes it a satisfying and comforting dish.

Coca de Trampó: Coca de Trampó is a traditional Mallorcan flatbread topped with a mixture of local ingredients, similar to a pizza or focaccia. The topping typically includes ripe tomatoes, onions, bell peppers, garlic, and olive oil. It is a simple yet delicious dish that highlights the freshness of the ingredients and is often enjoyed as a snack or appetizer.

These are just a few examples of the traditional cuisines you can find in Palma. The city's culinary scene is diverse and offers a wide range of dishes that celebrate the flavors of Mallorca and its rich gastronomic heritage.

Best Restaurants And Bars

Palma, the capital city of the island of Mallorca, Spain, offers a vibrant culinary scene with numerous outstanding restaurants and bars. Here are some of the best establishments in Palma that you should consider visiting:

Restaurants

Marc Fosh: This Michelin-starred restaurant features innovative Mediterranean cuisine with a focus on local and seasonal ingredients. It is located at Carrer de la Missió, 7A, 07003 Palma, Illes Balears, Spain.

Adrian Quetglas: Another Michelin-starred restaurant, Adrian Quetglas offers a contemporary dining experience with a fusion of Spanish and international flavors. Adrian Quetglas is at Carrer de Sant Feliu, 16, 07012 Palma, Illes Balears, Spain.

Canela: Known for its creative tapas and small plates, Canela provides a modern twist on traditional Spanish cuisine. Canela is at Carrer de Sant Joan, 4A, 07012 Palma, Illes Balears, Spain.

Forn de Sant Joan: Set in a charming old bakery, this restaurant offers traditional Mallorcan dishes prepared with fresh, local ingredients. Forn de Sant Joan is at Carrer de la Concepció, 12, 07012 Palma, Illes Balears, Spain.

Duke: With stunning views of Palma's harbor, Duke specializes in seafood and Mediterranean cuisine, accompanied by a vast selection of wines. Duke is at Paseo Marítimo, 29, 07014 Palma, Illes Balears, Spain.

La Bóveda: Located in Palma's old town, La Bóveda serves authentic Mallorcan cuisine, including delicious paella and fresh seafood dishes. La Bóveda is at Carrer de la Botería, 3, 07012 Palma, Illes Balears, Spain.

Ombu: This stylish restaurant offers a fusion of Asian and Mediterranean flavors, creating a unique and unforgettable dining experience. Ombu is at Carrer de la Concepció, 9, 07012 Palma, Illes Balears, Spain.

Ca'n Joan de S'Aigo: A historic establishment dating back to 1700, Ca'n Joan de S'Aigo is renowned for its traditional pastries, ice cream, and hot chocolate. Ca'n Joan de S'Aigo is Carrer de Can Sanç, 10, 07001 Palma, Illes Balears, Spain.

Bars

Abaco: Step into a magical world at Abaco, a bar adorned with extravagant decorations, flowers, and fruits. Enjoy a wide range of cocktails in a stunning setting. You'll find it at Calle San Juan, 1, 07012 Palma, Illes Balears, Spain

Sky Bar at Hotel Hostal Cuba: Located on the rooftop of Hotel Hostal Cuba, this trendy bar offers panoramic views of Palma while serving delicious cocktails and a vibrant atmosphere. Sky Bar at Hotel Hostal Cuba is at Carrer de Sant Magí, 1, 07013 Palma, Illes Balears, Spain.

Bar Flexas: A popular bar among locals, Bar Flexas is known for its extensive selection of craft beers and relaxed ambiance. Bar Flexas is at Carrer de Sant Magí, 26, 07013 Palma, Illes Balears, Spain

Bar España: Established in 1939, Bar España is a historic bar that exudes charm. It's a great place to enjoy traditional drinks and mingle with locals. Bar España is at Carrer de l'Almudaina, 2, 07001 Palma, Illes Balears, Spain

BrassClub: This elegant cocktail bar boasts a wide array of expertly crafted cocktails and a sophisticated atmosphere, perfect for a memorable night out. BrassClub is at Carrer de Sant Magí, 28, 07013 Palma, Illes Balears, Spain

Abacanto: Located in the heart of Palma, Abacanto offers a diverse menu of cocktails and an extensive selection of premium spirits in a stylish and contemporary setting. Abakanto is at Avinguda de Gabriel Roca, 29, 07014 Palma, Illes Balears, Spain

Bar Bosch: A classic meeting point in Palma, Bar Bosch is famous for its refreshing gin and tonic served in large balloon glasses. Bar Bosch is at Plaça Rei Joan Carles I, 16, 07003 Palma, Illes Balears, Spain

Rosa del Raval: Situated in Palma's vibrant La Lonja neighborhood, Rosa del Raval is a cozy wine bar that offers an excellent selection of local and international wines. Rosa del Raval is at Carrer de la Corderia, 16, 07002 Palma, Illes Balears, Spain.

These are just a few of the many exceptional restaurants and bars in Palma. Remember to check availability and make reservations in advance, especially for popular venues.

Also, the addresses are provided for reference and it's always a good idea to double-check the locations or use a navigation app for accurate directions.

Best Cafés

Palma is known for its vibrant café culture. Here are some of the best cafés in Palma that you can visit:

> *Rosevelvet Bakery:* Located in the heart of Palma, Rosevelvet Bakery is a popular café known for its delicious homemade cakes, pastries, and specialty coffee. The cozy atmosphere and friendly staff make it a great spot to relax and enjoy a sweet treat.

> *Cappuccino Grand Café:* Situated along the Paseo del Borne, Cappuccino Grand Café is an elegant café that offers a stylish and sophisticated ambiance. Known for its excellent coffee and delectable menu options, it's a perfect place for a leisurely brunch or afternoon coffee.

> *La Molienda:* La Molienda is a charming café tucked away in the narrow streets of Palma's Old Town. With its rustic decor and cozy atmosphere,

it's a great spot to savor a cup of expertly brewed coffee or try their selection of teas and homemade cakes.

Ca'n Joan de S'aigo: Established in 1700, Ca'n Joan de S'aigo is one of the oldest and most traditional cafés in Palma. This historic café is famous for its ensaimadas (a traditional Mallorcan pastry) and hot chocolate. It's a must-visit spot to experience a taste of Mallorca's culinary heritage.

Mama Carmen Café: Located near the Santa Catalina neighborhood, Mama Carmen Café is a trendy café known for its excellent coffee and delicious brunch options. The café has a modern and relaxed atmosphere, making it a popular choice among locals and tourists alike.

La Mémé: La Mémé is a hip café and bistro situated in the trendy neighborhood of Santa Catalina. Known for its creative menu and specialty coffee, this café offers a unique culinary experience. It's a great place to unwind, enjoy a cup of coffee, and savor their mouthwatering dishes.

These are just a few of the many exceptional cafés in Palma. Each café has its own unique atmosphere and specialties, so I recommend exploring different ones to find your personal favorite.

CHAPTER 5

SHOPPING IN PALMA

Palma offers an exciting shopping experience for locals and visitors alike. From popular shopping areas and markets to specialty stores and boutiques, Palma boasts a diverse range of options to cater to every taste and budget. Whether you're seeking souvenirs, local crafts, fashionable clothing, or unique finds, this article will guide you through the must-visit shopping destinations in Palma.

Popular Shopping Areas

Palma is home to several popular shopping areas that offer a mix of international brands and local shops. Here are some of the noteworthy areas to explore:

> *Passeig des Born:* Located in the heart of Palma, Passeig des Born is a bustling boulevard lined with upscale shops and designer boutiques. This tree-lined street is perfect for fashion enthusiasts looking for high-end brands.

> *Avinguda Jaume III:* Situated near Passeig des Born, Avinguda Jaume III is another renowned shopping street. Here, you'll find a mix of

international fashion brands, luxury stores, and jewelry shops.

Palma Old Town: The historic center of Palma, known as Palma Old Town, is a treasure trove of independent boutiques, quaint shops, and traditional stores. Stroll through the narrow streets to discover hidden gems and unique items.

Souvenirs And Local Crafts

To take home a piece of Palma's culture and heritage, explore the city's offerings of souvenirs and local crafts. Here are some recommendations:

Olivar Market: Located in the heart of Palma, the Olivar Market is a vibrant food market where you can also find local delicacies, artisanal products, and traditional crafts. Pick up some flavorful olive oil, handmade ceramics, or Mallorcan ensaimadas (a sweet pastry) as souvenirs.

Artesanía Textil Bujosa: This family-run shop specializes in traditional Mallorcan textiles, including woven fabrics, blankets, and decorative items. Each product reflects the island's rich textile heritage and makes for a unique souvenir.

La Pajarita: Situated in Palma Old Town, La Pajarita is a delightful boutique offering handmade leather goods, such as bags, wallets, and belts. Their products are crafted using traditional techniques, ensuring quality and authenticity.

Fashion And Design

Palma's fashion and design scene is diverse and vibrant, catering to a range of tastes. Whether you're seeking renowned international brands or local designers, you won't be disappointed. Here are a few places to explore:

Av. Jaume III and Passeig des Born: As mentioned earlier, these popular shopping streets are lined with fashion boutiques and designer stores. From high-end fashion labels to trendy clothing stores, you'll find an array of options here.

Rialto Living: Located in a beautiful historic building, Rialto Living is a concept store that combines fashion, design, and homeware. Browse through their curated collection of clothing, accessories, home decor, and gifts.

Cortana: This local designer boutique is known for its elegant, feminine clothing and unique designs. Cortana offers a range of ready-to-wear garments, including dresses, tops, and accessories.

Markets And Flea Markets

For a more authentic and vibrant shopping experience, don't miss out on the markets and flea markets in Palma. Here are a couple of notable options:

Mercat de Santa Catalina: This lively food market is a great place to immerse yourself in local culture. Apart from fresh produce and gourmet delights, you'll find stalls selling handmade crafts, jewelry, and clothing.

Rastro Palma: Held every Saturday near the Plaza Mayor, Rastro Palma is a flea market where you can hunt for antiques, vintage items, second-hand goods, and unique collectibles.

Specialty Stores And Boutiques

Palma is home to a myriad of specialty stores and boutiques that cater to niche interests and unique shopping preferences. Here are a couple of recommendations:

Perfumería Fiol: This exquisite perfume boutique offers an extensive range of locally crafted perfumes, scented candles, and beauty products. Discover your signature scent or find a thoughtful gift for someone special.

Patrícia Thomazo: If you're a fan of handmade jewelry, make sure to visit Patrícia Thomazo. This boutique showcases a collection of contemporary jewelry crafted with precious metals and gemstones.

Palma's shopping scene is a vibrant mix of popular shopping areas, local crafts, fashion boutiques, markets, and specialty stores. Whether you're looking for fashionable clothing, unique souvenirs, or one-of-a-kind items, the city has something to offer everyone. So, while exploring the charming streets of Palma, take the time to indulge in a memorable shopping experience that reflects the rich culture and creativity of the city.

CHAPTER 6

PRACTICAL INFORMATION FOR TRAVELERS

Here is some practical information to remember while planning a visit to Palma.

Money Matters

Currency:

The currency used in Palma, the capital city of Mallorca, Spain, is the Euro (€). It is advisable to carry some cash in Euros for small purchases and emergencies. Most businesses, including hotels, restaurants, and shops, accept major credit cards, but it's a good idea to have some cash on hand.

Money Exchange:

There are several options for exchanging currency in Palma. Banks and currency exchange offices are available throughout the city, including at the airport and popular tourist areas. It's recommended to compare exchange rates and fees before making a transaction to ensure you get the best deal.

ATMs:

ATMs are widely available in Palma, and they offer a convenient way to withdraw cash in the local currency. They can be found at banks, shopping centers, and popular tourist spots. However, it's essential to notify your bank before traveling to Palma to avoid any issues with your card being blocked due to suspected fraudulent activity.

Credit Cards:

Credit cards are widely accepted in Palma, including Visa, Mastercard, and American Express. Most hotels, restaurants, and shops accept card payments. However, it's advisable to carry some cash for smaller establishments or places that might not accept cards.

Language And Communication:

The official language spoken in Palma is Spanish, and it is widely understood and spoken throughout the city. However, due to its popularity as a tourist destination, many people also speak English, especially in hotels, restaurants, and tourist areas. It's always helpful to learn a few basic phrases in Spanish to communicate with locals and show respect for their culture.

Useful Phrases

Here are some useful phrases that you can use while in Palma:

1. Hola - Hello
2. Buenos días - Good morning
3. Buenas tardes - Good afternoon
4. Buenas noches - Good evening/night
5. ¿Cómo estás? - How are you?
6. Por favor - Please
7. Gracias - Thank you
8. De nada - You're welcome
9. Perdón - Excuse me/pardon me
10. ¿Habla inglés? - Do you speak English?
11. No entiendo - I don't understand
12. ¿Puede ayudarme? - Can you help me?
13. ¿Dónde está...? - Where is...?
14. ¿Cuánto cuesta esto? - How much does this cost?
15. Quisiera pedir... - I would like to order...
16. ¿Tiene algún recomendación? - Do you have any recommendations?
17. ¿Cuál es el mejor lugar para...? - What is the best place for...?
18. ¿Puede llamar a un taxi, por favor? - Can you call a taxi, please?
19. ¿Dónde puedo encontrar un banco? - Where can I find a bank?

20. ¿Dónde puedo encontrar un buen restaurante? - Where can I find a good restaurant?
21. ¿Dónde puedo encontrar una farmacia? - Where can I find a pharmacy?
22. ¿Cuál es la hora? - What time is it?
23. Necesito ayuda - I need help
24. Me gustaría reservar una habitación - I would like to book a room
25. ¿Puede recomendarme algún lugar para visitar? - Can you recommend a place to visit?

These phrases should be helpful in basic communication while in Palma, whether you're asking for directions, ordering food, or seeking general assistance.

Travel Insurance and Health Concerns:

It is highly recommended to have travel insurance when visiting Palma or any foreign destination. Travel insurance provides coverage for medical emergencies, trip cancellations, lost luggage, and other unforeseen circumstances. Ensure that your insurance policy covers the specific activities you plan to engage in while in Palma, such as water sports or hiking.

Healthcare facilities in Palma are of high quality, including public and private hospitals and clinics. It's advisable to have a valid European Health Insurance Card (EHIC) or appropriate travel insurance that covers medical expenses. Remember to pack any necessary prescription medications and consult your doctor before traveling to Palma, especially if you have any pre-existing medical conditions.

Safety And Security:

Palma is generally a safe city for travelers, but it's essential to take common-sense precautions to ensure your safety. Keep an eye on your belongings, especially in crowded areas, and avoid displaying expensive items or carrying large sums of cash. Stay in well-lit and populated areas at night, and be cautious of pickpockets in crowded tourist spots.

Travel Warnings:

Before traveling to Palma, it's advisable to check for any travel warnings or advisories issued by your government or the local authorities. These warnings provide up-to-date information on potential risks, such as political unrest, natural disasters, or health outbreaks. Stay informed and make informed decisions about your travel plans based on reliable sources of information.

Emergency Contacts:

In case of emergencies in Palma, it's crucial to know the local emergency contact numbers:

- *General Emergency: 112*

- *Medical Emergency: 061*

- *Police: 092*

- *Tourist Police: 902 102 112*

Make a note of these numbers and keep them accessible during your trip. If you encounter any emergency situation, contact the appropriate authorities immediately.

In conclusion, when visiting Palma, it's important to be prepared in terms of currency, language, and safety. Ensure you have access to Euros, consider having a mix of cash and credit cards, and inform your bank about your travel plans. Familiarize yourself with basic Spanish phrases, carry travel insurance, and take necessary health precautions. Stay vigilant, stay informed, and enjoy your visit to Palma, one of the beautiful destinations in Spain.

CHAPTER 7

CONCLUSION

In conclusion, Palma de Mallorca is a vibrant and captivating city that offers a perfect blend of history, culture, and natural beauty. From its stunning architecture to its golden beaches, there is something for everyone in this Mediterranean paradise. Throughout this travel guide, we have explored the city's top attractions, delved into its rich history, and provided useful tips to enhance your visit.

When planning your trip to Palma, it's important to remember a few key tips. First, be sure to explore the city's historic center, where you'll find landmarks like the Palma Cathedral and the Almudaina Palace. Take time to stroll along the charming narrow streets and discover hidden gems. Second, make sure to visit the stunning beaches, such as Playa de Palma and Cala Mayor, where you can relax and soak up the sun. Don't forget to indulge in the delicious local cuisine, with its emphasis on fresh seafood and Mediterranean flavors.

Additionally, we recommend exploring the surrounding areas of Palma. Take a day trip to the Serra de Tramuntana mountain range, a UNESCO World Heritage site, and enjoy breathtaking landscapes. Visit the picturesque village of Valldemossa, known for its charming streets and historic monastery. You can also explore the beautiful coastal towns of Soller and Port de Soller, with their stunning beaches and scenic train rides.

To make the most of your trip, it's essential to plan ahead and consider additional resources. Check out the official Palma de Mallorca tourism website for up-to-date information on events, attractions, and local recommendations. Utilize travel forums and online communities to connect with fellow travelers and get insider tips. Consider downloading a reliable travel app to have all the necessary information at your fingertips.

Finally, always remember to respect the local culture and traditions. Familiarize yourself with basic Spanish phrases to communicate with the locals and show appreciation for their way of life. Be mindful of the environment and follow responsible tourism practices, such as reducing waste and respecting nature.

Palma de Mallorca is a city that will leave you with lasting memories. Whether you're interested in history, culture, or simply relaxing on beautiful beaches, this Mediterranean gem has it all. By following the tips and recommendations in this guide and utilizing additional resources, you can ensure a memorable and enriching experience in Palma. So pack your bags, embark on an adventure, and let Palma de Mallorca captivate your heart.

Additional Resources

Below is a list of The Most Visited Travel and Tourism Websites which would aid you in finding whatever you need in regards to your travel to not just Palma, but anywhere else nationally and internationally. From accommodation arrangements to transportation bookings and everything else in-between, the following sites will assist you. Not all of the sites support Palma related aid, but a good number of them do.

1. booking.com
2. tripadvisor.com
3. airbnb.com
4. expedia.com
5. agoda.com
6. uber.com
7. southwest.com
8. jalan.net
9. aa.com
10. navitime.co.jp
11. vrbo.com
12. hotels.com
13. marriott.com
14. ryanair.com
15. delta.com
16. travel.rakuten.co.jp
17. makemytrip.com
18. kayak.com
19. united.com
20. skyscanner.net

21. irctc.co.in
22. tripadvisor.co.uk
23. thetrainline.com
24. hilton.com
25. rome2rio.com
26. bahn.de
27. trip.com
28. priceline.com
29. tutu.ru
30. flightaware.com
31. eastday.com
32. adanione.com
33. viator.com
34. latamairlines.com
35. klook.com
36. tripadvisor.in
37. ikyu.com
38. indianrail.gov.in
39. tripadvisor.it
40. tripadvisor.fr
41. easyjet.com
42. tripadvisor.es
43. ana.co.jp
44. tfl.gov.uk
45. jal.co.jp
46. travelandleisure.com
47. ihg.com
48. mta.info
49. aircanada.com
50. airbnb.co.uk

Printed in Great Britain
by Amazon